SURVIVING THE MEGATSUNAMI

by Madeline Tyler &
Sam Thompson

Minneapolis, Minnesota

Credits
Images are courtesy of Shutterstock.com. With thanks to Getty Images, Thinkstock Photo, and iStockphoto. Recurring images – mycteria, benchart, Andrii_Malysh, Bohdan Populov, Anastasiia Veretennikova, Francois Poirier, MaryDesy, vladimir3d. Cover – Zerbor, jakkapan, nayuki minase. 4–5 – Andrey Yurlov, Krakenimag-es.com, Bignai. 6–7 – Ryan Janssens, Semnic. 8–9 – Gareth_Bargate, Michael O'Keene, Jeka. 10–11 – tuna-salmon. 12–13 – Narongsak Nagadhana, lynx_v, Andrey VP. 14–15 – Simon Annable, Wang LiQiang. 16–17 –Anatoliy Karlyuk, Alex Izeman, Bruno Passigatti, Mike_shots, me_slavka. 18–19 – Darren Baker, Chatham172. 20–21 – Ronnie Chua, Mark Rademaker, Ivan Kurmyshov. 22–23 – austinding, Phonix_a Pk.sarote. 24–25 –john paul slinger, Fly_and_Dive. 26–27 – Ryan Janssens, Semnic. 28–29 – mimagephotography, Youkonton. 30–31 – PrimeMockup.

Bearport Publishing Company Product Development Team
President: Jen Jenson; Director of Product Development: Spencer Brinker; Managing Editor: Allison Juda; Associate Editor: Naomi Reich; Associate Editor: Tiana Tran; Art Director: Colin O'Dea; Designer: Elena Klinkner; Designer: Kayla Eggert; Product Development Assistant: Owen Hamlin

Library of Congress Cataloging-in-Publication Data is available at www.loc.gov or upon request from the publisher.

ISBN: 979-8-88916-593-4 (hardcover)
ISBN: 979-8-88916-598-9 (paperback)
ISBN: 979-8-88916-602-3 (ebook)

For more information, write to Bearport Publishing, 5357 Penn Avenue South, Minneapolis, MN 55419.

CONTENTS

A WALL OF WATER

How would you feel if the ground rumbled below your feet? What if you heard a rush of water?

If you are scared of the water, be warned . . .

IT'S A MEGATSUNAMI!

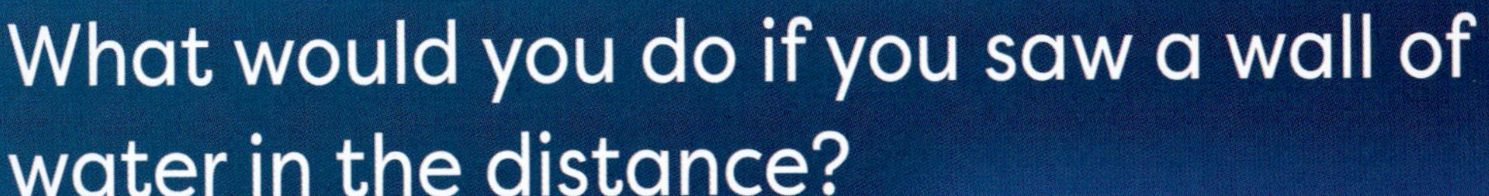

What would you do if you saw a wall of water in the distance?

It is time to become a megatsunami survival **expert.**

A tsunami is a series of giant waves. Once they reach land, they can be 100 feet (30 m) tall.

The waves can travel up to 500 miles per hour (800 kph). They crash on land minutes apart. This makes it hard to know when a tsunami is over.

How does a tsunami start? Earth is covered in huge rocks called plates. Sometimes, the plates grind and bump against one another.

The bumping can cause an earthquake. This pushes ocean water up and creates a tsunami.

SUPERSIZED TSUNAMI

Does a tsunami sound scary? Imagine seeing a megatsunami!

These waves are more than twice the height of a normal tsunami. Some would be taller than most buildings.

What might cause a megatsunami? If a lot of land slid down a mountain and fell into the sea, it would push the water up.

A large **meteorite** that hit Earth's oceans would do the same thing. It would create a big splash. That splash could become a huge wall of water.

Danger zones are places where tsunamis are likely to happen. The Ring of Fire is a danger zone in the Pacific Ocean.

It is an area where several of Earth's plates come together. Nine out of ten earthquakes happen here.

The largest recorded megatsunami happened in Alaska in 1958. It was caused by an earthquake that led to a **landslide**.

It made waves more than 1,600 ft (500 m) tall. Luckily, megatsunamis like this are rare.

STOP, LOOK,
LISTEN

How would you know a megatsunami is on the way?

One of the first signs is an earthquake or landslide. Can you hear a loud rumble? Is the ground shaking?

Turn on the news to hear what might happen next. Scientists who study tsunamis will use the news to warn you.

These experts are trained to notice patterns in the ocean. Make sure to listen for their warnings.

Are you near the sea? You can tell if a megatsunami might start by looking at the water.

Is water moving away from the shore? This is a sign that a giant wave is coming.

Check on your pets and other animals. Are they acting strangely?

Animals can sense when a tsunami is coming. Flamingos are known to flee before people even know what is going on.

TOOLS TO SURVIVE

Escaping a tsunami is dangerous. You will need to get supplies.

Soon, all the power will be off. Find a radio to stay up to date with the news. Get lots of batteries.

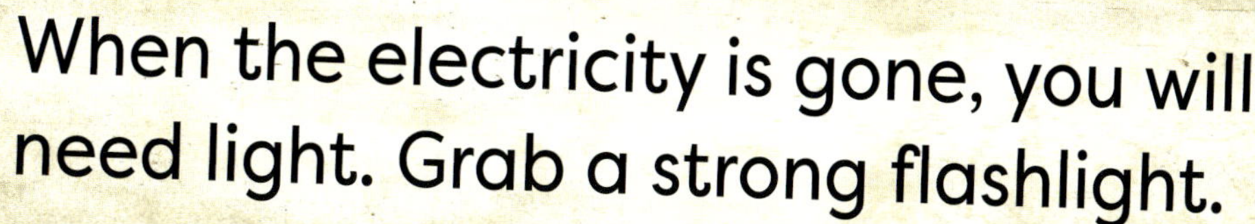
When the electricity is gone, you will need light. Grab a strong flashlight.

A first aid kit is a good idea, too. It needs to have bandages and **medicine** inside.

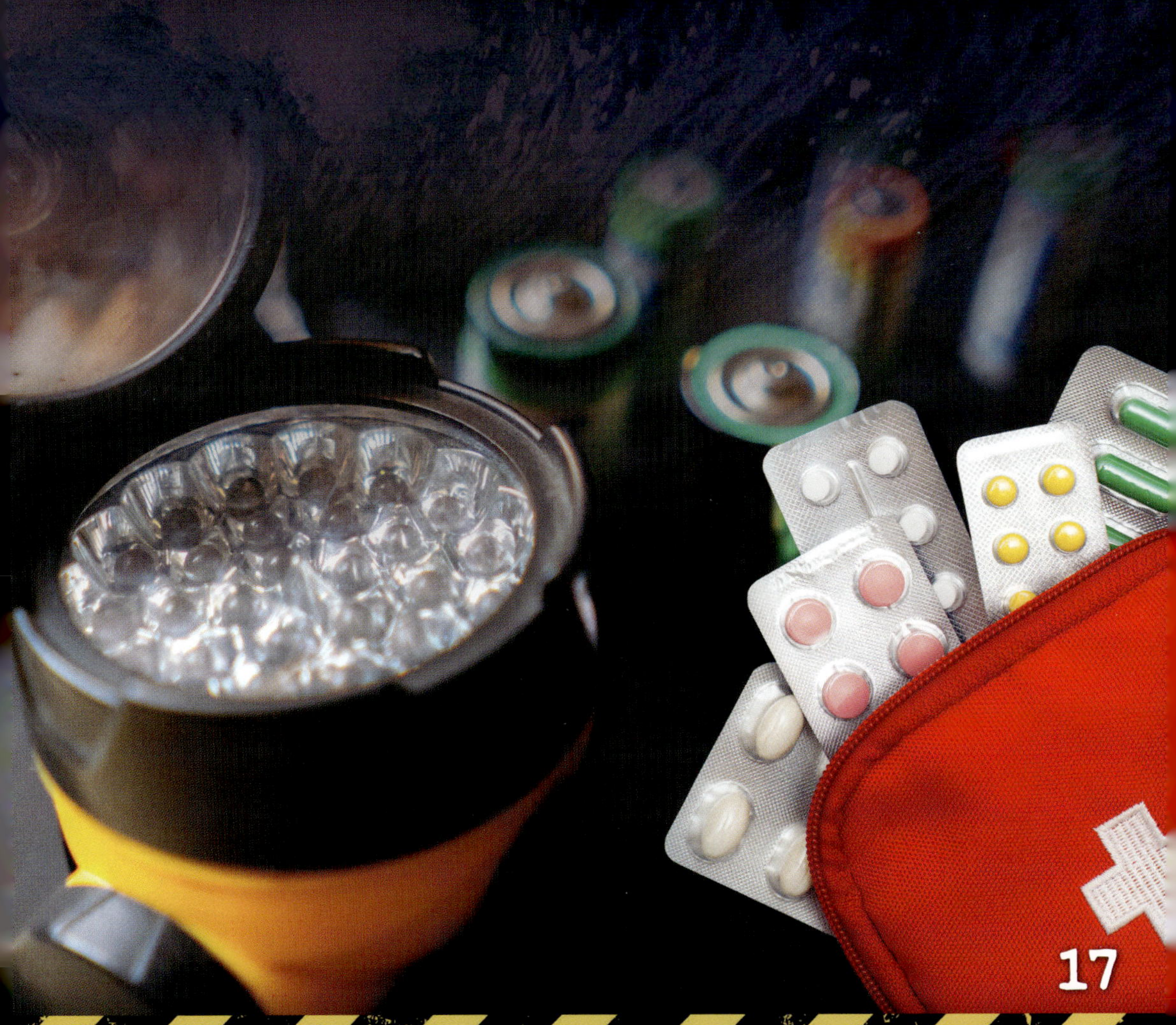

It will not be long before you get hungry. Get lots of canned food. Don't forget a can opener.

There are all sorts of canned foods. You might find beans, soup, or veggies.

Even though there may be lots of ocean water around, it will be salty. Do not drink salty water.

Fresh water in rivers and lakes could be dirty or salty from the big waves. Stay healthy by drinking bottled water.

ADVICE?

RUN!

Are you prepared? You will need to be faster than the giant wave.

Grab your survival kit. Head to safety with your family.

Is there a car around? Get in and drive quickly.

Get away from the coast and head inland.

The earthquakes and landslides that cause megatsunamis can damage roads and destroy buildings.

Watch out for broken roads. Stick to large, open spaces in case buildings fall over.

It is time to start heading up. You need to be high up to stay safe.

Try to get about 100 ft (30 m) above sea level. Keep climbing as high as you can. Then, get ready for a long wait.

YOUR NEXT STEPS

From high up, you can see everything happening down below. Wait there until the tsunami is over.

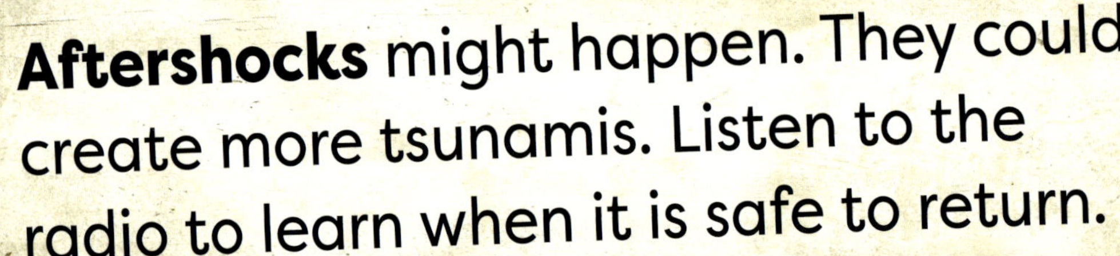

Aftershocks might happen. They could create more tsunamis. Listen to the radio to learn when it is safe to return.

Be careful when you go back to a city or town. Buildings might be weak because of the waves.

An aftershock could bring a building down at any minute. If you see a building shaking, move away quickly.

THE FALLOUT

Most of the roads around you will be damaged. It will be hard for people to travel.

You might not be able to find more food.

Even after the megatsunami has stopped, it is still dangerous. Your house could be underwater.

Try to find shelter somewhere else. Stay with other survivors.

Ration your food and bottled water. Try to make them last. You may not know when you can get more.

It may take time before the sea water drains away. Help others as you wait.

Cleaning up after a megatsunami could take years. But if you work together, it will be done in no time.

If you can face the force of a megatsunami, you can survive what comes after, too.

THE DISASTER CHECKLIST

How should you survive the megatsunami?

- ✓ Prepare a survival kit.
- ✓ Listen for earthquakes.
- ✓ Watch the water.
- ✓ Check on animals.
- ✓ Find a car.
- ✓ Head for higher ground.
- ✓ Wait until it is safe.
- ✓ Help others.

GLOSSARY

aftershocks smaller earthquakes that happen after larger ones

expert someone who knows a lot about a subject

landslide a large amount of earth and rock falling down a cliff or mountain, often caused by an earthquake

medicine something used or taken to fight off sickness or pain

meteorite a piece of space rock that hits Earth

ration to use in small amounts to save resources

INDEX

READ MORE

Taylor, Charlotte. *Terrible Tsunamis (Nature's Revenge)*. New York: Gareth Stevens Publishing, 2023.

Williams, Olivia. *Understanding Earthquakes and Tsunamis (Responding to Natural Disasters 21st Century Junior Library)*. Ann Arbor, MI: Cherry Lake Press, 2022.

LEARN MORE ONLINE

1. Go to **www.factsurfer.com** or scan the QR code below.
2. Enter "**Surviving Megatsunami**" into the search box.
3. Click on the cover of this book to see a list of websites.